LIMERICKS
ECLECTICA

LIMERICKS ECLECTICA

To Irwin —
Thanks for the help
and encouragement. At last!
Rod

RODMAN HILL

Library of Congress Control Number: 2014900706
ISBN: Hardcover   978-1-4931-6302-1
                 Softcover   978-1-4931-6301-4
                 eBook   978-1-4931-6303-8

Rev. date: 02/21/2014

To order additional copies of this book, contact:
Xlibris LLC
1-888-795-4274
www.Xlibris.com
Orders@Xlibris.com
540093

Introduction

by Cordelia Derhammer-Hill

These are limericks written over a span of years from about 2010 to 2013 by my father. I had asked him go back to working on his memoirs, of which he'd only ever written one chapter (now lost). He agreed, though reluctantly, but when I asked him if he'd been able to make a start, he showed me a limerick, instead. It seemed the more I hoped for personal narrative, the more he answered back in limericks.

They became something of a hobby. In fact, he told me, he would often wake up at 2 am with a limerick in mind, get to the computer, write it down, and then go back to bed. After a while, they were printed out in a continuously-updated, black 3-ring binder kept in the living room, from which he would regale guests with his creations, always to laughter, sometimes to blushes, and occasionally to deep mortification on the part of his family. Sometimes, requests to write verses including certain names were honored, with a special nod given to my mother, Naomi, and her penchant to shop.

When I asked him to tell me a little bit about the writing process, he had this to say,

"I was reminded of a game that some of my teenage cohorts
would play. We would, in turns, each sing a limerick that we
knew, interspersed with a chorus, and we would sometimes
go at it for an hour or more, before we had exhausted our
store of remembered verses."

Dad has taken a lot of trouble to include italicized words in each line
of most of his limericks, to make sure that people who are reading
them for the first time understand the flow of how the words are to
be read aloud. He also recommends reading them in small bites, not
too many at once. One last important note—Dad emphasizes that
these verses are not truly reflective of his personal obsessions, and
that he would not want anyone to mistake the subject matter as his
autobiography. For that, I am afraid we will have to keep pestering
him.

We hope you enjoy reading them—with laughter, blushes and
mortification—as much as we have enjoyed having them read to us,
and at least half as much as Dad has enjoyed writing them.

Cordelia Derhammer-Hill

Limerick *writing's* a worthwhile endeavor
If the *Limericks* are smutty or clever
Or *if* they're offensive
Or *make* you feel pensive
Or *if* they're . . . Oh whatever.

If *you* I offend, please excuse,
I *only* intend to amuse;
After *all's* said and done
You are the one
With *feelings* so easy to bruise.

I'm'n om*niv*orous and limerical predator,
What I *write* I take blame or take credit for:
Whether *Old* or Brand New,
Be it *Borrowed* or Blue,
I just *pray* it all gets by my Editor.

1. *Nymph*omaniacal Jane
    When *asked* about sex did exclaim,
    "There *isn't* much to it,
    You *just* have to do it
    A*gain* and again and again and again and again . . . . !"

2.   A *bare*footed hiker from Libya
De*cided* to walk to Namibia;
The ter*rain* was so rough
And the *trek*king so tough
That she *wore* her feet down to the Tibia.

3. *Too* many cooks spoil the broth
   And *too* many crooks roil my froth;
   But with *acts* much more heinous
   Some *Priests* flame my anus
   'Cause *too* many Cler'cs soil the Cloth.

4.　A *ped*erast priest from Peoria
　　While *tour*ing Boys Town intoned,
　　"Gloria In *Ex*celsis Deo!
　　What *else* can I say? Oh!
　　I'm *in* such a state of Euphoria!"

5.   De*gen*erate priests are abundant,
     With *al*tar boys often recumbent;
     These *Cler*ics, I find,
     Leave *no* boy's behind,
     To say "*ped*erast" priest seems redundant.

6.   A *three*-way: two gals and a guy
     Who were *ho*mo—and hetero—and bi-,
     Went *at* it so hot
     They got *tied* in a knot
     Took a *sail*or two days to untie.

7.   Naomi eschews cooking hominy
     To *her* that is such an ignominy;
     She'd *have* a few fits
     'Cause "*Put*tin' On The Grits"
     Would be *tres* gauche and so un-Naominy.

8. In a *broth*el, a cowboy named Tex
    Wore his *boots* and his spurs during sex;
    Whores' *yowls* and loud howls
    When they *spotted* his rowels
    Were out*match*ed when they heard him yell, "Nex'."

9.   An a*dult*erous Satyr named Muntz
     Was re*nowned* for his sexual stunts;
     In a *three*-way delicto
     He *asked*, "Where'd my dick go?
     It *must* be in one of your c_nts!"

10.   Fifty *times* Juan's been stopped at the border,
      An in*vet*erate Rio Grande forder;
      Getting *in*to El Norte
      'S not his *aim* nor his forte . . .
      It's an Ob*sess*ive Compulsive Disorder.

11. An un*fort*unate lass was Miss Bailey:
    To her *boy*friend she cried, "Waly, Waly!
    Your *f—king* lacks vigor,
    I *wish* you were bigger.
    And . . . *where* did you leave your SHILLELAGH?"

12. While *wear*ing his plaid Tam-O-Shanter
     A *Scots*man had no time for banter;
     With a *Pi*per-ish lilt
     He reached *in*to his Kilt
     And *fur*tively fingered his Chanter.

13. Three *broth*ers who hailed from Racine
    In *med*ical directions did lean;
    One be*came* a Podiatrist,
    And *one* a Psychiatrist,
    The *third* treated parts in between.

14. Multi*cult*ural and musical Veronica
    Observed *Christ*mas and Kwanzaa and Chanukkah
    Till *forced* to choose one
    Made it *no* longer fun
    So she *stayed* home and played her harmonica.

15. *Greta* Van Susteren's a wretch,
     She's a *mix*ture of Yenta and Kvetch;
     A *Shrew* and a nuisance
     Who *sticks* in her two cents
     And *makes* her neck something you'd stretch.

16. Without *shame* FOX TV brings us Hannity
    Who spews *lies* and his right-wing insanity;
    If *he* were done in
    It would *not* be a sin
    But a *boon* to the rest of humanity.

17. I wish *Lim*baugh, O'Reilly and Palin
     Had *tak*en a boat and gone sailin'
     To a *B*P oil spill
     Screaming, "*Drill*, Baby, Drill,"
     And *then* fallen over the railin'.

18. Pop ce*leb*rity's a social disease
     That in*duces* a sense of unease;
     The hys*ter*ical zeal
     Of *fans* makes one feel
     Like a *hound*dog surrounded by fleas.

19. I re*call* with deepest regret
     A re*ci*tal I've tried to forget;
     Yet I *still* feel dismayed
     Having *heard* Schoenberg played
     By a *Bag*pipe/Accordion duet.

20. She *said*, with words grossly inelegant,
    "Your *c-ck* is so small it's irrelevant."
    He said, "*Really?* Guess what,
    It's not *me*, you old tw-t,
    You'd be *loose* if you f—ked a large elephant!"

21. "GOTT IN *HIM*MEL!" What more could he say,
    His *flock* having moved far away;
    A*lone* on a stool
    In a *dark* empty shul
    Rabbi *Shmu*el kept moaning, "OY VAY!"

22. *My* most enjoyable sleep
    Begins *quick*ly and grows very deep;
    And if *I'm* not mistaken
    It *ends* when I waken
    With *no* appointments to keep.

23. "*Mary* was born without sin;
     Bore *Je*sus while still a Virgin."
     Not *doc*trines I'd stick to,
     Mir*a*bile dictu . . .
     But I *think* I'll recite them again.

24. Trans*vest*ites who live in Barbados
    Were *asked* by some men, "Will you date us?"
    They re*plied*, "If we do,
    Just be *warned* we don't screw . . .
    So for *sex* you will have to fellate us."

25. A *Boy* Scout, aggrieved and astonished,
    Did *good* deeds yet always got punished;
    He *fussed* and he cussed,
    "This *sh-t* just aint just!
    The *worst* I should be is admonished."

26. Some *signs* are a dead giveaway,
     One *should*n't ignore them they say:
     Shoes *mol*dy and musty?
     *Zip*pers all rusty? . . .
     It's *time* that you joined AA.

27. Out *West*, so an old Legend goes,
     And *how* it began no one knows,
     It *states* as God's truth
     That *Cow*boys are proof
     A*paches* once f-cked Buffaloes."

28. A *Cheese* that was named by a Punster
    Was dis*dained* and then thrown in a Dumpster:
    Part *Cu*ban, part *Jew*ish,
    Part *Liz*ard, quite newish,
    Called, "*HAV*A-NA . . . . GILA *MUEN*STER."

29. A *Bar*tender, feeling quite crabby,
    Hearing *jokes* from an off-duty Cabbie,
    Groaned, "*TELL* ME NO MORE!"
    When *in* through the door . . .
    Walked a *Past*or, a Priest, and a Rebbe.

30. *Us*ing their wits and their wiles
    They ap*proach* things with such diff'rent styles;
    Still . . . *Nan*cy Pelosi
    And *Bel*a Lugosi
    Have *one* thing in common: Their Smiles.

31. *Guests* were subject to delirium
    When *u*sing the hotel's Solarium;
    Now the *Gay*-Straight confusion
    Once *there* in profusion
    Is *gone*! Gays have found the A-Queer-i-Um.

32. His *tot*al inheritance's been spent
     And he *barely* recalls where it went:
     Drugs, *Whisk*ey and Song,
     A *Babe* in a Thong . . . .
     The *rest* he divested for Lent.

33. A *now* demised musical team
    Was com*prised* of thirteen Klezmorim;
    Each of *whom* strove to star
    As he *blew* his Shofar . . . .
    No one *want*ed to hear 'em or see 'em.

34.　Said an *In*dian Brave, and I quote him,
　　　"I *carved* my Squaw's head on my Totem;
　　　Yet she *could*n't construe
　　　That I *meant* to be true
　　　'Til I tat*tooed* her name on my scrotum."

35. With*out* a strong sense of the shoulds
    We *men* are mere babes in the woods;
    With *none* to direct us
    But *Penis* Erectus
    We're *all* just like Boyz in the Hoodz.

36. Ask *Ghet*to kids, "When's Fathers Day?"
     You'll *hear* them invariably say
     With*out* hesitation,
     "*Count*ing gestation,
     It's *nine* months before Mothers Day."

37. A *pole* dancer upped and confessed,
    "It's *easy* these days getting dressed:
    On *bot*tom a G-string
    That *cov*ers my Pee thing,
    On *top* . . . a diaphanous vest."

38. *Out*er-Space-Cold or Hell-Hot,
    E*mo*tion'l extremes were her lot:
    Whether *arc*tic or torrid
    She *was* very florid
    Ex*cept* when she slept . . . she was not.

39. Two gay men's _X_-Rated routine
    Got *even* more lewd and obscene:
    Stuck in *lock*step and nude
    They kept *wonder*ing *who'd*
    Crazy-*Glued* the god*damned* Vaseline?!

40. De*spite* all their contrary claims,
     They were *out*ed as gays by their names:
     Who *could* they outfox
     When *on* their mail box
     Was *writ*, "James Fitz*hugh*-Hugh Fitz*james*."

41. Was *GB* Shaw really a Jew?
Sans a *broad*-brimmed black hat . . . well who knew;
With his *beard* you might guess,
But a *Heebie* GBS . . .
Was be*yond* most people's purview.

42. An *angst*-ridden fellow named Keith
     Was *al*ways heard grinding his teeth
     'Til he *wore* them away,
     To his *dent*ist's dismay . . . .
     Now he's *grind*ing the gums underneath.

43. *Sex*, when it's woman-to-woman,
    Is a *spec*ial sensual communion;
    And it's *great* fun to watch
    Women *locked* crotch-to-crotch
    In a *Les*bian Labia Union.

44. Neither *Vam*pire, Werewolf, nor Ghost
    Could *find* a warm, welcoming host
    'Til a *Shade* started roomin'
    With *Har*ry S. Truman
    Whose "*DYB*BUK STOPS HERE" was his boast.

45. *Wedgies* make her *wiggle* and *dance*
    As *if* her butt's crawling with ants;
    There's *simply* no doubt
    She *must* pull wedgies out
    Or her *ass*hole will swallow her pants.

46. When a *sex*ual thirst you would quench,
    Find a *grass*-skirted, lap-dancing wench
    Who will *do* Hula Hula
    On *your* Big Bamboola:
    A*lo*ha! You'll feel like a Mensch!

47. His ne*fa*rious prank you must foil,
     His im*prac*tical joke you must spoil;
     So *I'm* telling you
     What *you're* not to do
     Is eat *On*ion Rings served by the Mohel.

48. His *op*eratic talents were various,
    His *six*-octave range not precarious:
    He'd re*cite* a Libretto
    Cas*trat*o Falsetto . . .
    And in *Bass*o Profundo sing Arias.

49. "For a *new* slant on life you should try us."
    Crowed *cock*-eyed Mohels Jed and Elias,
    "Our re*sults* are unique,
    They are *chic* and oblique,
    We make *all* of our cuts on the bias.

50. Most folks *crawl* long before they can walk
     And they *bawl* long before they can balk;
     Then, just to vex us,
     Some *folks* down in Texas
     Can *draaawl* long before they can talk.

51. Self-pro*claimed* "King of Pop" Michael Jackson
    When in *bed* with young boys kept his slacks on:
    He just *could*n't be "Bad"
    'Cause it *took* all he had
    Morphing *in*to a White Anglo-Saxon.

52. A *man* on his way to Utopia
    Stopped to *eat* at Cafe Cornucopia
    Where *hav*ing to squint
    At the *men*u's fine print
    Made him *think* he was in a Dystopia!

53. His *probe* the proctologist sneaked in
    As he *spread* patients' butt cheeks and peeked in;
    And the *doc* made them ponder
    Was it *doub*le entendre
    When he *asked* them, "Well, how was your Weekend?"

54. Some im*ped*iments you don't want to stop,
    Some af*flic*tions you don't want to drop:
    E.*g*., your Dyslexia
    Serves and protects ya
    Should you yell "CUFF YOU!" at a cop.

55. SHE was *trans*gendered into a HE
    And *that* was no small victory;
    The hard *part* of her task
    Was when *she* had to ask
    The *doc* for an . . . Adda*dich*tomy.

56. When *questi*oned, an athlete revealed
    A *drug* use he'd till then concealed:
    Claimed his *search* for enhancement
    Was *just* for romance meant
    And *not* for his play on the field.

57. An *old* agent's booking mistakes
    Left a *cli*ent with great pains and aches
    Who, in*stead* of a Lap Dance,
    Was *giv*en a Tap Dance
    That *turned* his balls into pancakes.

58. When you're *old* your hair mostly grows
      Out of your ears and your nose;
      One *raunch*y old goat
      Had *hairs* in his throat . . .
      How they *got* there you're left to suppose.

59. *Some* words are strictly taboo,
     Like "*G_D*" to an Orthodox Jew;
     You can *say*, "Motherf—ker,"
     Or "*Bite* me, C—ksucker!"
     Say the '*N*' word . . . it's curtains for you.

60. A *very* successful roue
    Made *con*quests with little delay;
    His *mere* introduction
    Sugges*t*ed seduction:
    "*Meet* Mister Roland De Haye."

61. A *shep*herd had only three ewes
    And he *didn't* know which ones to choose:
    *Be*ing a glutton,
    He'd *need* two for mutton . . .
    That would *leave* him just one to abuse.

62. Bill and *Mon*ica's ill-fated tryst
Was in*evit*able once he'd been kissed
Because *his* Oval Office
And *her* Oral Orifice
Were a *com*bo he couldn't resist.

Bill's a *Fox* and Ms Monica's a Chicken,
A young *intern* that he'd stick his dick in;
She *called* him "Timex"
'Cause *he* could have sex . . .
Take a *lick*ing and still keep on ticking!

63. *Beeth*oven's "Fifth" was inspired
    By a *wood*pecker's sound he admired:
    It's "*Peck*, peck, peck, *peck* . . .
    Peck, peck, peck, *peck*."
    Was *all* the help Ludwig required.

64. *Shad*rach, Me*shach* and A*bed*nego
   Es*caped* Babylon's fires many years ago:
   Were *they* here today,
   You *might* hear them say,
   "Global *Warm*ing! Let's *leave*! But where's *there* to go?!"

65. Of *all of* the Hookers I've known
 And *by* whom been balled or been blown,
 I'll *tell* you, by golly,
 There's *none* good as Molly
 Who's re*spect*fully called "Ho Malone."

66. The *stage* for sex is all set
    And *as* he gets hard she gets wet:
    They're *on* automatic
    With *no* prophylactic . . .
    I'll *bet* they're about to beget.

67. When he *farts* he prays out of his ass
    Come no *solids* or liquids, just gas;
    At his *age* he's uncertain
    But his *gut* sure is hurtin' . . .
    Que Se*ra* . . . Sera, it must pass.

68. On the *Lad*der That Leads to Success
    A *wo*man who wears a short dress
    Will *find* men won't mind her,
    They'll *line* up behind her.
    And *why*?. I'll bet you can guess.

69. When it *comes* to the fine art of screwin'
    Most men don't know what they're doin';
    They need *women* to train them,
    To *urge* . . . then restrain them,
    Or the *whole* f—king thing they will ruin.

70. A *strip* joint's larcenous star
    Pur*loined* all the tips in the jar;
    Last *seen* wearing scanties,
    Just *pasties* and panties,
    Dressed *so*, she won't get very far.

71. A *greedy* cow ate too much hay
And *then* had the Devil to pay;
The *cow* was quite moody
'Til *she* made a doody
And *let* the chips fall where they may.

72. On Mount *Rush*more make room for Obama,
    His *wife*, their two girls and his mama,
    And her *parents* who raised him,
    The *teachers* who praised him . . .
    They *all* deserve part of the glamma.

73. Norse god *Thor* came to Earth for a bit
    And he *bug*gered a cross-dressing Twit;
    When the *ham*-slam was o'er
    Thor *thund*ered, "I'M THOR!"
    "You're *thore* . . . I'm thow thore I can't thit!"

74. Broadway *Theater* would be a delight
      Were the *tick*ets not priced out of sight,
      And if *park*ing and meals
      Were *not* such big deals
      And the *god*damned seats weren't so tight.

75. An *idea* that's profoundly unpleasant
Claims, "There's *really* no time like the present:
Only *Future* and Hist'ry,
The *present's* a myst'ry,
And *Temporally* speaking, NOW isn't!"

76. *TWOS* want to run their own show;
     If you've *known* one you know that that's so.
     You can *thwart* such a hellion's
     Pre-school rebellions
     By *tell*ing him . . . "JUST SAY NO!"

77. We're not evolved and we're not a creation,
 We're an *extra*terrestrial invasion!
 Now *don't* feel insulted
 But *Hu*mans resulted
 From an *E*T-chimp miscegenation.

78. Had *Spitz*er and Woods met in REHAB
    They could've *had* themselves quite a good CONFAB
    Tryin' to *figure* out why
    The Ar*kan*san got by
    With a *WRIST* SLAP a WINK and a RIB JAB.

79. Financial High Lords lack lucidity,
    They *bank* on our widespread stupidity
    To *not* see their jobbery,
    Their *cons* and their robbery,
    Nor *no*tice their greed and cupidity!

80. About *noth*ing become sentimental
    Be it *Spir*itu'l, Physical or Mental:
    The *Limo*usine ride,
    The *Mate* by your side . . .
    Even *your* Lease on Life's just a Rental.

81. I be*lieve* cesspool cleaners are Saints,
    They *do* their jobs with no restraints;
    I *couldn't*, could you,
    Do what they do:
    Take *so* much shit with no complaints?

82. Black *Slav*'ry and Red Genocide
    Are not *mat*ters of national pride
    And they're *not* just the rhetoric
    Of *some* crazy heretic
    But *facts* from which we've tried to hide.

    Our *past* sins are painful to mention
    And to *do* so just causes dissention;
    But they *can't* be erased,
    And the *soon*er they're faced
    The *soon*er will come our Redemption.

83. OJ's *mur*derous crimes left him anguished,
　　　He'd an *un*conscious wish to be vanquished.
　　　Now his *guilty* obsessions
　　　And *veiled* confessions
　　　Have *stopped* since in jail he's languished.

84. To his *Fence* an old Gonif did say,
   "From this *heat* I am schvitzing avay;
   For a *dime* on the dollah
   I *vouldn't* hollah . . .
   It's *Too* Hot to Hondl today."

85. A *Salem* witch-hunter, with glee,
    Told *all* the townsfolk he could see,
    "When we *get* to the pyre
    Let *me* start the fire!
    Don't *try* matching witches with me."

86. In *Brooks* Brothers suits and bow ties,
     Three *Black* men, devoid of surprise,
     Had *already* guessed
     They would *hear* this request:
     "Will *all* three defendants please rise?"

87. Shakespeare's *Ham*let and Camus' Outsider
Sought to *leap* o'er the Life/Death Divider
But they *felt* so uncertain
'Bout *clos*ing Life's curtain
They let *some*one else be their Decider.

88. Going *South* on Route I-95
　　　Is a *Hell*ish and Nightmarish drive:
　　　You're sur*rounded* by HumVees
　　　Whose *drivers* are zombies
　　　So *old* they're more dead than alive.

89. With *Sun*glasses, Ball Caps and Shorts,
    Some Flo*ridians* think they're real Sports
    But their *Dress* Shoes and Knee Socks
    Re*veal* they are not Jocks,
    Just *guys* banned from Clay Tennis Courts!

90. *Oed*ipus, as he came of age
Had a *temp*er that none could assuage:
He got *in*to a lather
And *mur*dered his father
In the *old*est known case of Road Rage.

Although *Oed*ipus tried hard to duck her,
He and *she* got locked pucker-to-pucker.
What a *Fate*ful disaster!
He *married* Jocasta . . .
And be*came* the world's first Motherf—ker.

Patri*cidal*, Hubristic, Incestuous
And *rid*dled with guilt was King Oedipus;
Who *sought* expiation
Through *self*-mutilation
And the *scorn* he evoked from the rest of us.

To re*peat* this tale you needn't bother
Though it's *bet*ter than many another;
Whether *writ*ten or oral
This *tale's* got a moral:
"Be *sure* your girlfriend's not your mother!"

91. While *sail*ing through Romantic Climes
   O*dys*seus heard Siren's Chimes,
   "Have you *fall*en in love?" . . .
   "*No*! But, By Jove,
   I've *stepped* in it . . . numerous times.

92. Jesus *learned* from a Sophocles story
　　　How *Theb*ans were returned to Glory
　　　So as *man* not as God He
　　　Sub*ject*ed His body
　　　To *tor*ments quite painful and gory.

　　　Christ fore*stall*ed His Father's preemption
　　　By de*clin*ing a Princely exemption
　　　And by *Self*-sacrifice
　　　Paid the *ulti*mate price
　　　And *gained* Earthly sinners Redemption.

93. Do *I* pick up after my dogs?
    Yes . . . Un*less* they should poop during fogs
    Or when it snows
    And an *icy* wind blows
    That *turns* all of their turds into logs.

94. A *Strip*per of uncertain age
    Be*gan* her act nude on the stage
    And *then*, in small bits,
    Covered *Tush*, Twat and Tits
    Leaving *all* of the men in a rage.

95. A *paint*er of yore named Hieronymous
     Painted *peas*ants with pricks magnamonymous
     Thus en*rag*ing Patroons
     Whose *own* pantaloons
     Contained *pricks* . . . but none so enormanous.

96. A *Beach* Day can be a big fail-ya
    'Cause there're *so* many things to derail-ya:
    The *Sun's* cancerizers,
    A *Great* White's incisors,
    And *Teens* whose surfboards might impale-ya.

97. You *can*not stop Time so don't try,
    It *won't* even stop when you die
    And from your grave
    You *can't* cheer or wave
    At *Time* as it goes marching by.

98. A *Curse* left the Prince to bemoan
    That his *Princess'd* turned into a Crone;
    He was *told* not to weep,
    Beauty's *only* skin deep!
    "Yes . . . But *Ugly* goes down to the bone!"

99. With *tax* laws I'm in full compliance.
     On *me* you can have great reliance
     But *if* taking chances
     Could en*hance* my finances . . .
     I *might* risk a little defiance.

100. "Wear your *Thongs!*" cried the Topless Bar's boss,
     "If youse *don't* it could be a big loss:
     Thongs *do* double duty
     They *cov*er your booty . . .
     And *then* . . . they become anal floss."

101. What we're *doing's* a Crime and a Sin,
There are *so* many Laws it's agin
And I *pray* to Lord Jesus,
If *any*one sees us, . . .
They'll *simp*ly disrobe and join in.

102. When *Newt*, George and Bill went to see
     The *Wiz*ard in Em'rald City,
     Gingrich *asked* for a Heart,
     Bush *asked* to be Smart,
     And *Clint*on asked . . . "Where's Dorothy?!"

103. I wake *up* on the hour to Pee,
     You can *set* your timepieces by me
     But *don't* be misled
     I don't *get* out of bed
     Till it's *time* for my next Pot of Tea.

104. Lizzie *Bor*den's Black maid told her, "Missy,
      Ridin' *you* into town could cause mis'ry.
      To *drive* you I daren't . . .
      'Lessen *you* 'ax' your parents."
      What *Lizzie* did next . . . well it's Hist'ry.

105. The li*ai*son 'tween Tommy and Sally
　　　Couldn't have been more back alley
　　　Because *Jeff*erson and Heming
　　　Spent *day*times dissembling . . .
　　　Their *nights* they spent Down in the Valley.

106. His *Biz is* not bad as it looks
Because *Abie* keeps three sets of books:
For *buy*ing and selling,
What his *part*ners he's telling,
And *one* for those IRS crooks.

107. From be*tween* their two furry hind legs,
     Easter *Bun*nies lay choc-o-late eggs
     And *then*, so it seems,
     They pro*duce* jelly beans
     That are *made* from intestinal dregs.

     Feed *kids* all that crap if you'd rather,
     If *I* were you I wouldn't bother:
     The *Hal*loween Witch
     Is a *make*-believe bitch,
     And *Sant*a's her pedophile father!

108. The E*con*omy is in dissolution,
     It's a *prob*lem that needs a solution;
     We could *up* our employment
     And *sense* of enjoyment
     If we *legal*ized and taxed prostitution.

109. Maiden *Eve* was astroll in the Garden
        When she *first* espied Adam's huge hard-on:
        "If *I'm* not mistaken,
        That *looks* like a snake 'n'
        It's *sure* to displease the Old Warden."

        They knew their Boss wouldn't abide it,
        They got *scared* but remained undecided
        A*bout* what to do
        'Til *Eve* said she knew
        Of a *cozy* place where they could hide it.

        And *that's* how it all did begin,
        How we *got* in the trouble we're in:
        They started ballin',
        That *led* to the Fall 'n'
        Gave *birth* to Original Sin.

        Now a *God* like ours makes me feel wary,
        Does *God* have to be quite so scary?
        Why *doesn't* He chill . . .
        Take a *toke* or a pill?
        Better *still* . . . He should go and shtupp Mary.

        A *sched*ule like His keeps Him busy
        And at *times* it must make Him feel dizzy;
        At the *end* of His *day* who
        Is *there* He can *pray* to? . . .
        He's The *High*est of *Pow*ers! . . . or *is* He?

110. A *Savings* Bank teller with morals
        Showed no *int*erest in Bon Bons and Florals:
        When you *wooed* her she'd grin
        At *what* you put in
        But she'd *frown* at your early withdrawals.

111. Mary *Ann*, Matil*da* and Miss *Dor*ot'y,
     Saga *girls* with of*fici*al aut'ority,
     Can *lay* in the sand
     Or in *surf* they can stand
     Doing *tricks* they learned *in* their Sorority.

     Sigma *Ep*silon Chi is its name
     And *spread* far and wide is its fame:
     A Greek-*Eng*lish translation
     Needs *no* explanation,
     S-E-*X* either way is the same.

112. She *went* from too *fat* to ethereal
      Eating *noth*ing *but raw* whole grain cereal;
      When, *not* of her choosing,
      She *could*n't stop losing.
      She *went* from too *thin* to fun*er*eal.

      Ano*rex*ia will give you the Blues
      After *all* the good food you refuse,
      You'll be*come* Skin and Bones
      And your *star*vation 'Jones'
      Will *leave* you with nothing to lose.

113. At *first* just with eyes did they flirt
Till he *put* his hand under her shirt
But *what* made it certain
That *they* were through flirtin'? . . .
His *mus*tache went under her skirt.

114. *One* day his passion just dwindled
     Leaving *her* feeling sexu'ly swindled;
     His loss of lust
     Made Vi*a*gra a must
     And *thus* might his lust be re-kindled.

     He said, "*Darl*ing, it isn't your fault
     That our *lovemaking's* come to a halt;
     My e*rect*ile dysfunction
     Has *caused* a disjunction:
     I can't *open* your vaginal vault."

     When she *did*n't respond to his flattery
     He *asked* her, "Dear, *what* might the matter be?"
     She re*plied*, "I don't know
     Why I *feel* so low . . .
     Oh . . . My *vi*brator needs a new battery."

     He was *thought* to be typic'ly fickle
     'Cause his *passion* had ebbed to a trickle;
     But the *sad* fate of men
     Is that *they,* now and then,
     Simply *need* a new fancy to tickle.

That's why *mag*azines like Hustler and Playboy,
De*pict*ing the latest in Girl Toy,
Arrive *month*ly, not annu'ly,
To *help* men do manu'ly
The *thing* that they greatly enjoy.

Then *men* are aroused and excited,
Their li*bid*os become re-ignited;
With their *new* Stroke Book Issues,
A *full* box of tissues . . .
They *could*n't be more self-delighted.

'Til the *thrill* of the new sensuality
Is *felt* to be a triviality;
That's when *they've* had enough
Of the *fant*asy stuff
And men *yearn* to return to reality

115. A *man* meant to *pee* in a bucket
　　 But he *missed* and pissed *in*to a socket,
　　 Whose *Two*-Twenty Volts
　　 Gave him *such* painful jolts
　　 He lit *up* like a July Fourth rocket.

116. He *can't* see as good as he used-ta,
     He *mis*took a Hen for a Rooster;
     When the *bird* didn't crow
     At the *dawn*ing's first glow
     He *took* a beanpole and he goosed her.

     Oh *my*! How the feathers did fly,
     That *fowl* tried to peck out his eye!
     And the *hen* was not chicken,
     She *pulled* out the stick 'n'
     Said, "*Now* give my front hole a try!"

117. *Frank*ie and Johnny were lovers
     And they *swore* to the Heavens above us
     To be *true* to each other
     But *John*ny, that Mother,
     Was *found* under Nellie Bly's covers.

     There was *noth*ing that Johnny could say
     So he *knelt* down and started to pray;
     But *Frank*ie was sore
     And with *her* Forty-Four
     Blew phil*and*ering Johnny away.

     It *wasn't* just his Hanky-Panky
     That *made* an assassin of Frankie:
     What made her shoot?
     He was *wear*ing the suit
     That she'd *bought* him . . . now *that* made her cranky.

     So *lads* if it should come to pass
     That you're *caught* corking some other lass,
     Don't *count* on contrition
     To *cure* your condition . . .
     Use *Kev*lar to cover your ass.

118. Eve and *Ad*am had their share of trouble
      So did *Betty* and her Barney Rubble
      And *Rom*ulus and Remus,
      Who *were* in extremis,
      'Cause *all* of their trouble was double.

      Then there were Bonnie and Clyde
      Who *roamed* a depressed country side
      Like *Butch* and Sundance
      They *hadn't* a chance . . . .
      Ain't it a shame how they died?!

      Thel*ma* and Louise had a yen
      To es*cape* the harsh tyranny of men:
      They ran *off* in a car,
      But they *did*n't get far,
      So they *drove* the car off the deep end.

      Desde*mona* and Moorish Othello,
      Pre*cur*sors to Ni*cole* and her fellow . . .
      O*J*-what's-his-name . . . ?
      Of the "*gloves*-don't-fit" fame . . .
      Who now *sits* and has fits in his cell-o.

119. *Glut*tony he couldn't curtail
     Made him as fat as a whale;
     If some *weight* he could work off
     Each *time* that he'd jerk off . . .
     He'd *soon* be as thin as a rail.

120. There are *things* that don't make a good blend,
     They yield *out*comes you didn't intend:
     A *man* mixed Cialis
     With *some* old Vitalis
     And *now* his hair's standing on end.

     He be*came* even more of a wreck
     When he *used* his Viagra to check . . .
     If *mixed* with List'rine . . .
     Well *I've* never seen
     A *man* with a stiffer stiff neck.

121. A *speech* defect made him a lisper
     Who *only* could talk in a whisper;
     His *soft* breathy sound
     Drew *one* gal inbound
     And *when* she got close . . . well he kithed her.

122. Brooklyn *Gay* Bars don't want interlopers,
     You know . . . *guys* who complain about gropers,
     Who when *asked*, with no foolin',
     "May *I* push your stool in?"
     Think they've *just* met some courteous Slopers.

     A *Reg*ular can get somewhat furious
     When he *hits* on a guy who's 'just curious'
     And his *wish* to befriend
     Comes *to* a dead end . . .
     That could *make* the flirtatious . . . injurious!

123. Geese *gather* together in groups
      And they *cover* large fields with their poops;
      You'll soon *hear* someone swear,
      "Get the *flock* out of there
      And *lock* up their asses in coops!"

124. Your *Lib*erty is easily destroyed,
     A con*di*tion that you can avoid
     By *just* being diligent,
     E*tern*ally vigilant . . .
     But *then* you'll be called paranoid.

125. E*rect*ile Dysfunction's a curse
     But a *four*-hour hard-on is worse:
     When *broads* hear about it
     Your *bed*room gets crowded
     With *hordes* that you cannot disperse.

     They *all* want a piece of the action
     With a *man* who has one main attraction:
     Put his *ass* on a pillow,
     Voi*la* . . . Human Dildo!
     What's *more* . . . They're assured satisfaction.

     Yo*him*bine, Viagra, Cialis
     Are *drugs* used to prop up the phallus;
     Yes, they *can* help your schlong
     Get real *hard* and last long
     But be*ware* . . . don't develop a callous.

126. A *couple* that lived out in Boise
When *doin'* it were more than just noisy:
They *were* so frenetic
And *so* energetic
You could *hear* their wild frenzy in Joisey!

127. A *steel*-driving man named John Henry,
      To es*cape* obsolescence and penury,
      Chose to *race* a steam drill
      To a *drop* dead standstill
      In a *con*test that defined a Century.

      At *first* it did seem a disaster,
      'Cause the *steam* drill worked cheaper and faster;
      John should *not* have competed
      Nor been *seen as* defeated
      Because *man's* no machine . . . he's its Master!

      Now we *all* feel John Henry's unease
      As our *jobs* disappear overseas
      And it *causes* nervousness
      When *our* goods and services
      Are pro*vided* by Czechs and Chinese.

      Since our *jobs* have gone over the boundary
      It's no *won*der that we're in a quandary;
      But *have* no misgiving,
      We'll *still* make a living . . .
      By *taking* in each others' laundry.

128. You can *hear* right wing activists cry
That the *min*imum wage is too high
And *if* you're not wealthy
Or *don't* remain heathy
They *say* you're too old when you die.

Hey! What *hap*pened to Social Security
And its *prom*ises for our futurity?
. . . It se*cures* a safe niche
But *just* for the rich
While they *wait* for their gold bonds' maturity.

129. She was *jaded* and couldn't enjoy
      Having *sex* with a man or a boy;
      The *hor*rible fact was
      She *need*ed a cactus
      To *use* as a sexual toy.

      If the *cac*tus was coated with prickles
      She could *feel* intromission as tickles
      And she *said*, "When I'm horny
      I *need* something thorny
      'N' more *fun* than a barrel of pickles."

      Then she *met* a war Vet amputee
      Who had *one* leg cut off at the knee;
      His er*ogenou*s stump
      Gave to *her* such a hump
      She's still *glow*ing in post-coital glee.

130. There *once* was a powerful Queen
Who was *known* far and wide to be mean;
Using *int*imidation
This *Queen* cowed a nation
And *no* protestation was seen.

The *Queen* knew where bodies were buried
And *that* made so many folks worried:
Just the *threat* of exposure
Or de*struct*ive disclosure . . .
And *straight*way for cover folks scurried.

But the *Queen* too had secrets to hide
For the *Queen* did not feel bona fide:
Though not *easy* to see
The *Queen's* family tree
Had been *tar*brushed a bit on the side.

The Queen's *dresses*, silk stockings, and heels
Were *put* on to see how it feels
To *look* like a woman,
To *act* less inhuman,
And to *shriek* and emit girlish squeals.

You *knew* the Queen: J. Edgar Hoover,
A *Bur*eau Chief shaker and mover
Who *in*vestigated
The *ones* he most hated . . .
The *rest* were not part of his oeuvre.

Yet he *wasn't* safe from attack
Since his *und*erlings, behind his back,
Called him '*J.* Niggar Hoover'
Or '*Gay* Edgar Hoover'
And *that*, I must say, is a fac'!

131. It's a *mat*ter of some notoriety
That a woman showed great impropriety
When she *let* loose a fart
That made *every*one start . . .
Now she's *no* longer seen in society.

If a *man* had performed the same thing
They'd've *let* all the Town Hall bells ring;
They'd have *been* celebrating
His *loud* flatulating
While *Choruses* his praises would sing.

Well, *so* much for gender equality,
Where *wom*en are known for frivolity,
And must *act* with gentility
From *birth* to senility
While *men* have the lion's share of jollity.

132. Maiden *Mary* was said to be virginal,
    Because *none* of her sins were original;
    Meaning *she* had no new ones
    Just *old* tried and true ones,
    Not *crim*inal but nonetheless seminal.

133. Holy *men* demand women be seen
     To be *virg'nal*, enshrouded and clean;
     Other*wise* it is said
     They'd be *bet*ter off dead
     Then their families they couldn't demean.

     That's why *women*, when thought to have sinned,
     Are *beaten* until they are skinned,
     Then *they* are disowned
     They are *spat* on and stoned
     Till their *men* feel no longer chagrined.

     What *God* condones such mad behavior
     That *makes* of Man Woman's enslaver?
     If He *thinks* it's okay
     To *act* in that way
     Then *God* too has need of a Savior!

134. He *thought* that by flashing his c-ck
       Most *wom*en would recoil in shock
       So *it* really pissed him
       When *wom*en dismissed him . . .
       "Where's the *rest*, did you put it in hock?"

135. She asked, "*How* can I know I exist?"
As an *old* French horn player she kissed;
He said, "*You'll* know you're real
As *you* start to feel
My *fist* up your bum to the wrist!"

136. When *chorus* girls Trixie and Mitzi
    Dated *men* who were wealthy and ritzy,
    They *nev*er gave in
    To those *opulent* men
    Until *given* some gems that were glitzy.

    If at *first* their boyfriends were tight-fisters
    The *girls* were like virtuous sisters;
    Till the *guys* had epiphanies
    That *sent* them to Tiffany's
    Where they *bought* the girls gleaming arm-twisters.

137. Syba*rites*, for their third anniversary,
     Had some *surgery* that wasn't just cursory:
     She re-*shaped* buns and boobs
     And they *both* tied their tubes
     Leaving *them* a playpen but no nursery.

138. A *gay* man at first was nonplussed
When his *late* lover's urn he did bust;
Then he *thought*, "It's not tragical,
In*deed* it's quite magical:
I'm *covered* with his Fairy Dust!"

139. It's called *wax* if it comes from your ear,
   If it *comes* from your eye it's a tear;
   But *just* think of this:
   They are *called* shit and piss
   When they *come* from your front and your rear.

140. Did I *moan*, "O, no, no?" No, Naomi did!
   But that's *some*thing about which I am prone to kid
   So with *thought*ful reflection
   And *some* retrospection
   Read the *first* line again, it's a *quo pro quid!*

141. In a *wheel*chair propelled by a nurse
     He *felt* his life couldn't be worse
     Till he *hap*pened to glance
     At a *man* in a trance
     As an*other* went by in a hearse.

142. *Trans*cendental Meditation
    Beats *Psych*otropic Medication:
    If you're *suggestible* and numb
    And your *mantra* is "KUM,"
    Then it's *just* like a Club Med vacation.

143. For six *months* John received the wrong hormone,
     He got *est*rogen 'stead of testosterone;
     When *he* shrieked in terror
     His *Docs* found their error . . .
     They *winced* at how small both his balls had grown.

     Adding *insult* to injury's the pits:
     John was *forced* into wearing loose knits
     And the *dough* he was saving
     Since *he* had stopped shaving
     Was *spent* on bras for his new tits.

144. Phila*delph*ia, so I've heard it said,
  Is the *home* of folks very well bred
  And there's *really* no doubt
  Philly's *nicely* laid out
  But *who* knows how long it's been dead!

145. A *native* New Yorker named Percy
      Cried *out* to the Heavens for mercy,
      "I've *lost* my way,
      And I *hope* and I pray
      That this *road* leads to Hell . . . not to Jersey."

146. His *wife's* on a three-week vacation
Yet *he* has no fear of starvation:
Like *any* old geezer
He'll *eat* from the freezer . . .
But *where* will he get aggravation?

147. The *Ultra* Right relishes prosperity
      For them*selves* and for all their posterity.
      As for the rest of us . . .
      They'd have the best of us
      Heading for ultra austerity.

      They think *Government's* too big and too greedy,
      That it *caters* too much to the needy . . .
      So they'll *use* budget axes,
      Cut *spending* and taxes,
      Then *they'll* from the Union secede-y.

148. He *hung* in his shower room locker
      Pix of *Boop*, Grable, Davis, and Crocker;
      It seemed *foo*lish and petty
      But *wom*en named Betty
      Just *knocked* him right off of his rocker.

149. A man *thought* that he'd entertain us
    With be*haviors* both odious and heinous
    By *fart*ing nonstop
    Until *we* called a cop
    And a *Judge* ordered sewn shut his anus.

    *Doc*tors won't need gloves or glasses
    To *find* where the hole in his ass is:
    They can *just* light a match
    And then *stand* back and watch
    For the *source* of the bright flaming gasses.

150. In *China* they rarely make chili
And they *seldom* make china in Chile;
Two *facts* quite absurd,
And *here* is a third:
In chin*chilla* you never feel chilly.

151. A nude *Hombre* and a bare-assed Muchacha
      Were *doing* a horizontal Cha Cha
      When she *cried,* "Ay Caramba,
      Let's *switch* to a Samba,
      This *Cha* Cha's too fast for my Chocha."

152. At his *age* having sex made him grunt,
      'Twas like *doing* an acrobat's stunt;
      An arth*ritic* attack
      Gave to *him* a stiff back
      When he'd *rather* have had a stiff front.

153. It *just* wasn't Dracula's wont
　　　To take *love* sips from old Sappho's fount
　　　But Drac's *willing* assistant
　　　Was *not* so resistant
　　　And *gladly* went down for the Count.

154. Old *Tom* had his swimming pool deepened
And the *Life*guard upon whom he'd depend
Told him, "*With* your fragility
And *creep*ing senility
You should stay out of the deep end.

155. A *poor* man had no pot to piss in
     And *that* wasn't all he was missin':
     He *kept* snakes as pets
     Which *caused* him regrets
     'Cause *he* had no pit they could hiss in.

156. *Ann* Coulter's bitchy demeanor
    Makes it quite hard to demean her.
    She e*mits* evil vibes
    With her *harsh* diatribes . . . .
    To de*mean* her you'd have to be meaner.

157. His *sex* life was weirdly exotic:
     Ambi*dex*trously autoerotic;
     Then his *right* hand found out
     What his *left* was about . . .
     The *jealousy* drove him psychotic.

158. It's said *auto*erotic asphyxia
      Is a *Than*atos-Eros admixture;
      You have *no* way of knowin'
      If you're *coming* or goin' . . .
      And the *prac*tice is subject to stricture!

159. Clarence *Thom*as . . . Now where did they find him?
In some *Hell* devils must have designed him;
He's a *fascistic* fool
And an *anti*-Black tool,
Here's the *proof*: rabid racists don't mind him.

160. There *once* was a man from Wisconsin,
     Neither *rich* nor particu'ly handsome,
     Who could *bone* any chick
     That *he'd* deign to pick:
     He was *thought* to possess a huge johnson.

     But Hugh *John*son was his proper name,
     Not a *genita*l size claim to fame;
     Still each *gal* he would bed
     Cried that *she'd* been misled
     And mis*laid* in a Bait-and-Switch game.

161. She'd not *let* his cock near her pudendum
     Un*less* it was clad in a condom
     But his *aller*gy to latex
     Meant *they* would have no sex
     And *that* made their lives less than humdrum.

     Till he *found* a discarded silk stockin'
     And *made* a sheath to wrap his c-ck in,
     Covered *that* with a rubba,
     Then *howled*, "Hubba hubba!" . . .
     Last *heard* they were rollin' and rockin'.

162. A wild *Upper* West Sider named Whitney
     Would c*avort* on the ol' Hampton Jitney;
     It *made* me feel sad,
     She was *wantonly* baaad
     'N' there was *sex* to be had . . . but I'd'n gitney.

163. Echo *stood* with her back to a mirror
     Facing *Nar*cissus standing quite near her;
     She thought *his* loving glance
     Upped their *chance* for romance . . .
     Well she *couldn't* have been more in error.

     Nar*cis*sus, he just loves Narcissus,
     For *no* one else does he have kisses;
     His *lust*ful Libido's
     Ca*thect*ed his Ego:
     He's *Mister* Narcissus . . . and Missus.

164. It was *Mardi* Gras and just for the hell of it
Jane de*cided* she'd not remain celibate:
"I'll just *let* Lust hold sway,
Freely *give* sex away . . .
But on *second* thought . . . maybe I'll sell a bit."

165. From their *conf*lict there's been no surcease,
     No Is*raeli*-Palestininian peace,
     Just *end*less successions
     Of *leth*al aggressions
     That *do* not show signs of decrease.

     One *side* wants a sovereign nation,
     The *other* fears annihilation.
     Is there *no* resolution
     Ex*cept* dissolution
     That *ends* in a mad conflagration?

166. A *veteran* comedian was told
That his *jokes* were too clean and too old;
He re*plied*, "Well . . . f-ck you!
I *ain't* working blue,
Not for a sh-tpot of gold!"

167. A re*ligious* young woman named Britney
      Would at *first* not get cuddly and kitteny;
      But she'd *soon* get excited
      Once you'd recited
      A *Book* of Common Prayer litany.

168. Some *Christ*ians feel great guilt and shame
And are *not* quite sure who they can blame:
"Is God *try*ing to tease us
By *making* Lord Jesus
A *Jew* . . . with an Hispanic name?"

They *couldn't* believe in Him wholly
Yet His *halo* did make Him look holy;
Nah! . . . The *true* Son of God
Would *not* look so odd
And have *both* hands and feet quite so holey.

169. A Chi*cana* en route to Chicago
　　 En*count*ered a Customs embargo
　　 Where a *full* body search
　　 For il*legal* drug 'merch'
　　 Turned her *into* a raging Virago.

　　 "Chu *wan'* me to strip an' spread what?!!
　　 Oye *mira*! I ain' no slut!
　　 An' I *ain'* no drug mule
　　 So jes' *bese* mi culo,
　　 Chu *ain'* messin' 'roun' in my butt!"

170. If *you* would be healthy and lean
     Eat real *food*, not too much, mostly green;
     Use *meat* as a condiment
     And *not* the preponderant
     Part of your daily cuisine.

171. A *mari*juana plantation's peons
    Are *still* singing praises and paeans
    Since they *found* 'twas no joke
    They'd get *all* they could smoke
    'N' lieu of *pesos* their boss had been paying.

    And *if* they got hungry or tired
    They *knew* they could be re-inspired
    By *tak*ing a hit
    From the *dyn*amite shit
    That they *grew* . . . . that was all they required.

172. If to *Heaven* you go when you die
You will *float* on a cloud in the sky
'Til your *cloud* turns to rain
And it *flows* down a drain . . .
Then you'll be left high and dry.

173. *Bella*, the Belle of Biloxi,
　　　Wed a *Death* Row con (that really shocks me).
　　　The *next* thing she did
　　　Was she *bore* him a kid
　　　Con*ceived* not by him but by proxy.

174. Old *Harv* and his girlfriend were scroon
     But *no* one knew what they were doon
     'Til some *son* of a bitch
     Upped and *flipped* on the switch
     Let'n' light *Shine* On . . . Shine On Harvey's Moon.

175. A*bor*tions to her are horrific,
    Contra*cep*tion far less than terrific;
    So it's *rather* bewild'ren
    She *has* just two children:
    Well . . . She's *strictly* pro-life . . . not prolific.

176. *Young* Sophie's therapist's couch
    Was the *site* of her sexu'l debauch:
    Her *trans*ference, his counter-,
    Im*pelled* him to mount her
    And *charge* for those sessions . . . that slouch.

177. She's flir*tatious* and skimpily dressed,
     Still men's *passes* made her feel distressed:
     "Why're they *hitting* on me
     I *just* cannot see . . . .
     Could it *be* something that I've repressed?"

178. *Suze* has the Blues or she's Manic,
     She's de*pressed* or she's deep in a panic;
     Sue's a *bi*polar Queen
     With no *mood* in-between:
     She's An*gelic* and then she's Satanic.

     To *Suze* you're a giant or a midget,
     She's as *loose* as a goose or she's rigid;
     She's *sure* to confuse you,
     For *when* Suzy screws you
     She's *multi*-orgasmic or frigid.

179. A *man* consumed naught but legumes
 Then e*mitted* the foulest of fumes
 And *when* the man died
 His stink *didn't* subside . . . .
 He's in*terred* in the deepest of tombs.

180. Being *neat* and as fit as a fiddle,
     At *urinals* I aim for the middle;
     Thus I *deep*ly abhor
     Those slobs *who've* gone before
     And *left* the floor covered with piddle.

181. There's a *dental* assistant named Frances
Who *no* longer takes any chances:
By a *patient* once bitten,
She *now* wears her mittens
When she *makes* oral cavity entrances.

182. I like *air*lines that don't overbook.
     I like *food* that chefs don't overcook.
     But I *like* most of all
     For the *gals* that I ball
     All my *short*comings to overlook.

183. *Henry* and Anne were out strollin'
      When he *said*, "I think I'll take you bowlin'."
      She said, "*As* I recall,
      We *don't* own a ball." . . .
      "Don't *worry* 'bout that, Mistress Boleyn."

184. The sat*yri*asis of a cocksman from Natchez
     Had him *skew*ering young women in batches;
     Their tight *snatch*es, I hear,
     Caused him *such* wear and tear
     That his *prick* is now plastered with patches.

185. She'd *yet* to've been licked or been kissed
      By a *well*-practiced cunnilinguist
      And her *new*-found French lover,
      So *sad* to discover,
      Was a *vaude*villian ventriloquist.

      As his *head* slithered down to her tummy
      She ex*pected* the sex to get yummy;
      But *something* was wrong,
      The head *didn't* belong
      To her *beau* it belonged to his dummy.

      She got *mad,* "That French bastard, how could he
      Have mis*read* and so misunderstood me?" . . .
      Now her *nouveau* amigo's
      Her *beau's* alter ego:
      A *dummy* . . . who packs a big woodie.

186. A *small* group of sinister senators,
    Who are *right* wing extremist progenitors,
    *Us*ing hypocrisy,
    As*sault* our democracy
    With the *fury* of carniv'rous Minotaurs.

187. A bor*dello's* entire female crew
    Upped and *quit* without saying adieu;
    So the *mad*am did bawl
    As *johns* came to call,
    "Gents, . . . I *only* have guys for you."

188. Kind Pau*lette* was a pussy purveyor,
     For a *paltry* price she'd let you lay her
     And *if* you were broke
     She would *still* let you poke
     But you'd *have* to provide all the labor.

189. In a *move* that was unprecedented,
     To the *Royal* Court old Abe was presented:
     As he *knelt* to be knighted
     Abe *felt* so excited
     He *pissed* the striped pants he had rented.

190. Anne He*donia* used sex just for breeding;
    To her, *fore*play meant hours of pleading.
    She'd say, "*F-ck*ing's no fun,
    Let me *know* when you're done,
    I would *like* to get back to my reading."

191. An *inter*faith pair in distress
     Found a *chapel* that eased their duress:
     Neither *Cath'*lic, nor Jewish,
     Ecu*men*ic'ly newish,
     Called "Our *Lady* of Perpetual Tsures."

192. There *once* was a gay man named Jack
      Who would *now* and then make a wisecrack:
      If bending *over* you feared,
      He might *say*, "Dont be scared
      And don't *worry* . . . . I've got your back."

193. Many *movie* stars have mansions near Hollywood;
     Stars in *India* have palaces near Bollywood;
     And in *digs* just as classy
     A drag bitch named Lassie
     Re*sides* in a kennel called Colliewood.

194. Folk mus*icians* are not up to par,
     Not the *ones* I've heard playing so far:
     They spend *half* their time tuning,
     And the *other* half ru'ning
     Their *songs* with an untuned guitar.

195. In the *throes* of a mid-winter blizzard
       Horny *Liz* chose to visit her Wizard;
       As she *reached his* boudoir
       She just *froze* . . . how bizarre . . .
       A *Witch'd* turned him into a Lizard.

       Then the *Witch* turned Liz into a Cat
       Who *purred* to herself, "Fancy that . . .
       I'm so *furry* and sweet,
       Is there *nothing* to eat?
       Meow . . . that *Gecko* sure looks nice and fat."

196. Consider this young hooker's offer:
     For the *pitt*ance you put in her coffer
     She'll *ten*derly suckle
     *Un*der your buckle
     Then *tick*le your bum while you boff her.

197. Most Re*pubs* wanted Willard to stop
     Making *bids* to be their ticket's top;
     They *wished* for a nom'nee,
     *Some*one not Romney . . . .
     They *feared* 'Mitt the Flipper' would flop.

198. Rick San*to*rum is holier than thee,
He *has* no Church/State boundary.
In his *ex*postulation
He *claims* copulation
Is *work* and not play (or should be).

199. Po*litical* campaigns always worsen
When there's *even* just one ruthless person
So Re*pubs* had no doubt
They were *better* without
Newton *Leroy* Gingrich, ne McPherson.

200. Liber*tarian* Ronald John Paul
     Wants *gov*er'ment to be oh so small
     That if *he* we elec'
     To be*come* Chief Exec
     He'd pre*side* over nothing at all.

201. What *two*-legged animals f-ck Cats
     Yet are *fearful* of spiders and bats?
     From *what* I have seen
     There's *Missus* Levine . . .
     And *even*, at times, Missus Cats.

202. An *un*trusting Knight had to ask
     That his *Smith* do the following task:
     "Fit my *wife's* pubic pelt
     With a *chastity* belt . . .
     And her *face* with a chastity mask."

203. Despite *doses* of Bayer and Bufferin
      Lizzie's *cold* had her laid low and sufferin'
      'Til she *found* an elixir
      That *shortly* did fix her:
      A *chicken* soup called Bubbeh-myosin.

204. *Whether* it's thick or it's thin
    Black folks have slow-aging skin
    Because *in* their integ'ment
    There's *found* a rare pigment
    They *lovingly* call "Watermelanin."

205. Abie *went* to the garden to pee
     And got *stung* on his shlong by a bee;
     'Tween the *pain* and huge swellin'
     We'd *no* way of tellin' . . .
     Was he *yellin'* . . . or k'velen with glee?

206. Sadie's *daughter's* three husbands were doc-tahs,
     Each one *rich* from a lucrative prac-tahs
     'Til her *daughter* divorced them
     And, *boy*, what it cost them . . .
     One *daughter* but . . . Oy! . . . so much nachas.

207. Mad Docs *Frank*enstein, Jekyll 'n' Moreau
     Shared a *prac*tice 'cause business was slow;
     They split *fees* with each other
     And *went* even fu'ther . . .
     They split *patients* . . . . How low can you go?

208. At an *orgy* where Hedda first met us
　　She *swore* she would never forget us;
　　So we *asked* to do more
　　Of what *we'd* done before
　　The big *quest*ion was . . . would Hedda let us?

209. Listen *Gents*, if you relish good lovin',
Take it *slow*, don't go pushin' and shovin';
As a *baker* once said,
"For good *sex* or good bread,
It's important to pre-heat the oven."

210. He'd have *gone* to the john a bit oftener
Had he *found* an effective stool softener
And if *his* anal aperture
D'not *shrunk* to a miniature
Of *what* it had been . . . when 'twas open-er.

Bowel im*paction* can no longer worry him
Nor *cause* painful strains and delirium;
From a *laxative* OD
He just *died,* happily,
And *when* he stops shitting they'll bury him.

211. At the *salon* where my hair is dressed,
     Where it's *curled*, permed, relaxed or processed,
     I can *leave* my old rut
     By just *having* it cut . . .
     Departed, unlocked or distressed.

212. Even *though* they were sister and brother,
     A bi-*gal* and bi-guy wed each other;
     To *add* to their sins
     They *also* were twins
     With trans*sexu'ls* for father and mother.

     All the *fruit* on their family tree
     Was as *strange* and deranged as could be
     'Cause each *woman* and man
     In that *ill*-fated clan
     Was a *multiple* pers'nality.

     First to *waken* each morning would try
     The three *others* to i-den-ti-fy
     By *grab*bing one person,
     Start *scream*ing and cursin',
     "Who'n Hell're *you*? . . . Who are they? . . . Who am I?"

213. Lyndon, *Jim*my, Jack, Bill and Barack
Put A*meri*ca on the right track;
Dick, *Ron* and the Georges,
Those po*liti*cal scourges,
Are *guys* Willie Mitt would bring back.

214. "Job Cre*ators*" all yearn to be free
    To *manage* our e-con-o-my;
    Before *they* run the show
    I think *we* ought to know
    Just *how* they pronounce "J-O-B."

215. He was *only* a humble coal porter
      Who on *hot* days would quaff a cold porter;
      Then he'd *make* like Astaire,
      Do a *dance* debonair
      While he *crooned* a tune writ by Cole Porter.

      One *hot* day a talent scout spotted him
      And *into* a musical slotted him;
      Now he's *shed* his coal dust
      For a coat of *gold* dust
      And for *fame* that was once not allotted him.

216. If over *working* is one of your schticks
     You're a *candle* with too many wicks;
     To *be* at your best
     You must *now* and then rest . . .
     Even *God* just works 24/6.

217. It *drives* him right over the fringe,
    And it *just* makes him whimper and cringe:
    He quivers and quakes,
    Gets a *case* of the shakes
    If he *sees* a nurse with a syringe.

218. If *drug* companies all had their way
     There would *soon* be a new holiday:
     One where *men* would be rigid,
     En*gorged*, hard and turgid
     From *pills* they took on . . . "Erection Day."

219. In the *Village* on Christopher Street,
　　　That's *where* the effete meet to eat
　　　And where *dykes* in black leather
　　　Com*pete* with each other
　　　For *femmes* just as gay . . . more discreet.

　　　A *bus*load of big-butted butches
　　　Met a *large* batch of bosomy bitches;
　　　Took'm a *while* to discover
　　　They could *all* ball each other
　　　And *that's* when they stripped off their britches.

　　　Using *tongues* and thumbs, fingers and lips
　　　They mas*saged* and licked A-holes and clits;
　　　When at *last* they were through
　　　They just *bid* adieu
　　　With a *sisterly* kiss on the nips.

220. There *was* a Pulaski Day Princess
      Who ate *Horse*radish/Limburger Blintzes:
      Gave her *breath* an aroma
      That *could* cause a coma
      So to *freshen* up she used garlic rinses.

221. A *jealous* old man from Duluth,
      In a *desperate* quest for the truth,
      Water*boarded* his wife
      Within an *inch* of her life . . . .
      She thought him rather uncouth.

222. A mu*cha*cha who hailed from Caracas
     Liked to *rattle* and shake her maracas;
     If you *got* her excited
     She'd *be* quite delighted
     To *rattle* and shake her whole carcass.

223. An in*somniac* who went to the opera
     Could *not* have been any improper-er:
     When the *over*ture started
     He *slept*, snored and farted . . .
     And *that* made him very unpopular.

224. Righteous *female* monkeys in threes
Are *often* seen sitting in trees:
Hands on *ears*, eyes and mouth,
(Not on *parts* further south)
Thank *God!* They can still spread their knees.

225. A *bird*-loving gay man named Lou,
     In the *birdhouse* at his local zoo,
     Fed his *favorite* parrot
     A *garden*-fresh carrot
     Then *lovingly* . . . kissed a large cockatoo.

226. Careless *Maisie*, asleep on a chaise,
  Was *hoping* that she'd catch some rays:
  Rav'nous *birds* did detect her,
  Flocks *swooped* down and pecked her . . . .
  For *sun*block she'd used mayonnaise.

227. A Cha*sid* told his wife that he feared

People would think they were weird

If, *due* to some hex,

They should *die* during sex

And their *bodies* were found beard-to-beard.

228. While *troll*ing a beach on Antigua
    A *saga* boy, feeling quite eager,
    Was *hoping* he'd find
    A blond, *gen*'rous and kind,
    Who'd re*spond* when he tried to intrigue her.

    But he *quickly* sank into a funk:
    The *gals* all preferred other hunks
    'Cause the *rolled* up gym sock
    He'd stuffed *in*to his jock
    Had *slipped* to the rear of his trunks.

229. A rich *miserly* Scot from the Highlands
    Moved to the Hebrides Islands;
    Though his *wealth* was quite vast
    He re*mained* so tight-assed
    That *if* he ate coal he'd shit diamonds.

230. A *type* two diabetic, not sick,
     Had a *male* member both long and thick;
     His *nurse* wondered could she,
     W*ould* she, or should she . . .
     Prick his *finger* . . . or finger his prick?

231. You've *no* need for balls made of brass
     Nor a *penis* that none can surpass:
     Gals will *think* that you're hot
     Just as *long* as you've got
     A *hard*-hitting, pile-driving ass.

232. Knowing *Shy*sters from Roosters's no art,
   You *don't* have to be very smart:
   One *clucks* his defiance
   And *one* f-cks his clients . . . .
   That's *how* you can tell them apart.

233. A *hand*some young fellow named Bigelow
     Be*lieved* that he'd be a good gigolo:
     From waist *up* he was buff
     But that *wasn't* enough . . .
     Because *Bigelow* was not very big below.

     Rich *Cougars* wants more for their dough
     Than a *Dandy* or Arm-Candy beau:
     A *lover's* crotch bulge
     Should dis*creetly* divulge
     That he's *huge* . . . yet still able to grow.

234. An Hawaïan-Korean-Colleen
Was called *KoKo*, aka Kathleen;
She could *paint* a la Titian
But be*came* a physician
Who'd *scant* time for art in between.

She'd a *pallet* knife and brush in a jar
Near an *easel* outside her OR;
Her an*esthe*tized patients
Had *oodles* of patience
And *were* her best models by far.

235. *Hypo*chondriacal Louise
     Can i*mag*ine she has a disease
     And pre*sent* with the syndrome,
     Have *every* known symptom
     And *suffer* intense agonies.

     Lou*ise* sees her doctors as heroes
     Whose *pills* cure her ills (far as she knows);
     And *though* it seems mean,
     To her *doctors* she's seen
     As the *ulti*mate Queen of Placeboes.

236. Into *bed* with each other we hop,
     We have *fun* yet we know when to stop:
     There are *bodily* spasms
     And *tingly* orgasms . . . .
     (Oh, for *signals* like that when we shop).

237. For Tom, *gals* at the bar were too highbrow,
    When *he'd* say Hello they'd say Bye now . . . .
    But he's *no* longer spurned
    Since the *gals* have all learned
    Tom can, *using* his tongue, touch his eyebrow.

238. A Dee *Aitch* takes Bob's turn at bat,
     Designated *Drivers* chauffeur his Fiat;
     When it *comes* to love-makin' . . .
     Bob's *wife's* not forsaken
     There's a *Desig*nated F-cker for that.

239. *Ego*maniacal Donald,
    While *selling* junk bonds he had bundled,
    Made some *real* estate deals
    That he *saw* as real steals
    And then *crowed* 'bout the way he had hondled

    There is *always* another young blond'll
    Try *getting* her hands on "The Donald"
    But *soon* they all find
    That *they've* been screwed blind
    And been *cheated*, bamboozled and scoundrel'd.

    Don's a *latter* day Davey Croc-*kett*,
    Keeps a *bleached*-blond raccoon for a pet;
    With lips *pursed* and cheeks pouty
    There *isn't* a doubt he
    ... *Wears* his raccoon <u>*sur sa tete*</u>.

240. His *dick* gets so hard none can match it,
     He can *use* his man part as a hatchet;
     And *I've* heard him tell,
     When it *reaches* full swell,
     That *even* a cat couldn't scratch it.

241. A young *woman* was very housebound,
     And had *no* way of getting around
     Till her *boy*friend, named Mike,
     Gave to *her* his old bike
     Now she *pedals* herself . . . all over town.

242. Bar girl *Vicki* was slipped a few Mickeys,
      She a*woke*, her neck speckled with hickeys . . . .
      Looked like *Vlad* the Impaler
      Been *trying* to nail her
      Or *seamen* just looking for quickies.

243. A *whore* can't surrender control
     To a *john* she picks up on the stroll;
     If she *does*, on a whim,
     He'll want *her* to pay him
     For their *obvious* reversal of roles.

244. Rebs con*vened* once they heard the Pig Caller
Summon *them* to a conjoint 'waller'
Where they *swore* to be true
To their *Red*, White and Blue:
Red*neck* and White Trash and Blue Collar.

245. J. San*dusky* for boys had a yen
        Just to *butt* rape a few now and then;
        He *was* interdicted,
        Got tried and convicted,
        Then sent from Penn State to State Pen.

246. Gun *lobbyist* Wayne LaPierre
     Would like *guns* to be found everywhere;
     And *if* that were done
     Some*one* should shove one
     Right *up* Lapierre's derriere.

247. There *once* was a lassie named Minnie
     And, a*las*, she was ever so skinny
     That she'd *need* a plush cushion
     To *sit* her thin tush on
     Or *else* when she sat she'd sound tinny.

     Minnie's big sis was named Mattie
     Who, *as* you would guess, was a fatty;
     Side by side, now and then,
     They looked like a ten
     But apart, caused remarks that were catty.

248. A *hard*, horny cocksman named Smith
     Was *lauded* in legend and myth:
     When he *knocked* on a door
     Gals knew *what* he knocked for
     And what's *more* they knew what he knocked with.

249. A *new* bride with passion did burn
Un*til* she was startled to learn
That her *bride*groom was bi-
And *that* made her cry . . .
Poor girl *didn't* know which way to turn.

250. A *mon*strous Nebraskan named Jerry
     Was *fat*, *tall*, Neanderthal-hairy;
     He shed *mounds* off his butt
     Then he *had* his hair cut
     And *now* doesn't look half so scary.

251. Abo*rigines* in Central Australia
     Are so *proud* of their male genitalia
     While *ambling* about
     They *let* them hang out
     As *part* of their tribal regalia.

252. Re*morse*ful and penitent Berenice
    A*toned* climbing up the Pyrenees;
    To as*sure* being forgiven
    She was *shorn and was* shriven
    Then *made* the ascent on bare knees.

253. On a *res* lived an old Potawatomi
     Who, for *pot*, would perform acts of sodomy;
     When folks *ran* out of pot
     She'd cry, "*What* else you got? . . .
     You know *I'll* work for 'shrooms if you *gotany*."

254. His *navel* abutted her spine,
    His *lap* wrapped around her behind;
    When *asked*, "Whatcha doin'?"
    He *said*, "We're just spoonin'
    But *forking's* what I had in mind."

255. There *was* a young man from Calcutta
     Who *smeared* his bare buttocks with butta,
     Not to *prep* for a bash
     But to *soothe* a harsh rash . . . .
     Now *get* your mind out of the gutta.

256. An hor*olo*gist, a kind of clock doc,
      Was *called* on to treat an ill clock;
      When *old* clocks got sick
      And *only* could tick,
      He had *ways* . . . of making them tock.

257. A *very* rich man from North Africa
     Was a *sex* slaves and opium traffica;
     His bor*dellos* and dens
     Satis*fied* depraved yens . . . .
     I'm reluctant to be any graphica.

258. In *Congress*, where conflict's the rage,
Pols *fight* like bears locked in a cage;
While the e*conomy* it wrecks,
When it *get* down to sex,
Just *hope* they're not on the same Page.

259. There's a *lovely* young gal from Astoria
     Whose *beauty* and charm cause euphoria;
     To *her* it's been said,
     "Get your *folks* back in bed
     'Cause we *want* them to make a few more-a-ya."

260. Stu *sat* on the steps of his stoop
      Where he *sought* to sip some of his soup;
      The *super'd* been mean,
      Hadn't *swept* the steps clean . . .
      Stu got *soot* on the seat of his suit.

261. Bald Bill *rushed* to the chapel to pray
     For *he* had the Devil to pay;
     But 'twas *no* help because
     God knew *not* who he was:
     Bill'd for*got* to put on his toupee.

262. A *hybrid* lab's docs did devise
    A *bio*-genetic surprise:
    Crossed a *mule* with an onion
    And *got* from that union
    Some *ass* that brought tears to their eyes.

263. Count *Dracula*, while serving guests meals,
　　 Made *special* ingestion appeals:
　　 "It *matters* a lot
　　 If your *toddy's* not hot,
　　 So *drink* it before it congeals."

264. It *seems* that police have gone wild
     As they *stop* and frisk those they've profiled:
     If you're *black* or you're brown
     They can *just* pat you down
     And then *leave* you there feeling defiled.

265. He's a *one*-eyed, one-legged high seas pirate
     With a *flint*lock but he fears to fire it;
     The *first* time he tried,
     The gun *made* him one-eyed
     And i*rate* . . . so he had to retire it.

266. An e*state's* old gatekeeper named Roy
Greeted *costume* ball guests with great joy
Till he *found* at the gates
A *nude* man on skates
Who de*clared* that he was a pull toy.

267. If you *want* to go drugging and fressing,
    One-stop *shopping's* a Heaven-sent blessing:
    You'll get *food*, drugs and all
    In an *East* Village Mall
    At their *new* Psychedelicatessen.

268. Errol, a *swash*buckler, wielded a cutlass
     As he *rend*ered his enemies nutless;
     In a *count*er attack,
     When *Errol* turned his back,
     His *foes* left him lying there . . . buttless.

269. Popeye, *spotted* by Mickey and Pluto,
      Was *seen* eating only prosciutto;
      Mick said, "*Finish* your spinach
      Or your *strength* will diminish
      And you'll *get* an ass-whipping from Bluto."

270. Hookers *Scarlett*, Carlotta and Charlotte
       Plied their *ven*'rable trade at a car lot;
       When they *got* you inside
       You could *go* for a ride
       In a *hot* car and in a hot harlot.

271. A young *actress* complied with tradition
     And she *went* to a private audition
     Where the *casting* director,
     With *his* meat injector,
     Put *her* in an awkward position.

"I *didn't* come here to get laid,
I *came* for a part to be played
So if *you* put your pole
Any*where* near my hole
I ex*pect,* for that role, to get paid.

The pro*ducer*, too, tried to seduce her
Thought by *now* that she'd be a bit looser,
That she'd *take* on the part
Of a *real* backstage tart . . .
He got *slapped* when he just tried to goose her.

Now she's *one* of those celebrities,
Whom *others* she tries hard to please
And she *owes* her success
To her *talent*, I guess,
And t'what's *done* on her couch and her knees.

272. There's an *old* Roman god we call Janus,
    Whose du*plicity* has made him quite famous;
    So ... *what's* his fame's basis? ...
    This *god* has two faces,
    Two *cocks* and a two-barreled anus.

273. Snow White's *dwarfs* all had such evil twins
      That they *slipped* naive Snow Mickey Finns
      And when *they* sang 'High Ho'
      They *meant* stuporous Snow
      Was a*vailable* for various sins.

      There was *Rock*, Gropey, Hashmule and Greasy . . .
      And *Crappy* and Frumpy and Sleazy;
      They got *caught* pimping Snow
      And to *jail* they did go
      Singing, "*Life* Without Disney's Not Easy."

274. Freud's *shortest* analysis by far
    Was with *someone* who felt below par,
    Who said, "*I'm* in a jam,
    I don't *know* who I am."
    Freud asked, "*Who* doesn't know who you are?"

275. Aerialists Annette and Louise
      Did their act on the highest trapeze
      'Til one *day*, on a bet,
      They dis*pensed* with their net . . .
      Now Annette flies alone . . . ill at ease.

276. A Nor*wegian* collegian named Lars
     Was *often* seen sleeping in bars
     Where *folks* thought it best
     T'*l*et the *chug*alugger rest.
     Other*wise* he might sleep . . . driving cars.

277. A *high* school's new Driving Ed teacher
       Had a *student* and he did beseech her
       To *please* drop his class
       For he *feared* that his ass
       Would be *lost* due to that klutzy creature.

       She *couldn't* tell her right from her left,
       Her *color*blindness left her bereft:
       Couldn't dis*tinguish* between
       Red, amber or green . . .
       In *short*, she was anything but deft.

278. John was *offered* a piece of hair pie
     Which he *turned* down and I'll tell you why:
     He'd just *come* from the gym
     And a *nude* co-ed swim
     And had *had* a box lunch at the 'Y'.

279. For a *com*munications mishap
Liz *gave* her new girlfriend a slap.
Liz said, "*I* am a Thespian,
Not *some* lisping Lesbian,
Now *get* your face out of my Lap.

280. An e*vent* can be mystical or lyrical,
     Be hys*terical* or even satirical,
     Ir*rational*, inane,
     In*telligent,* insane . . .
     If *it* creates faith it's a miracle.

281. A *symbiotic* trio I know
        Are a *Vice* Cop, a Pimp and a Ho
        Who re*ly* on each other
        Like *sister* and brother
        To *screw* the johns out of their dough.

282. There are *times* when I just want to cry,
     As a *dirge* becomes my lullaby
     And the *memories* I keep
     Sadly *lull* me to sleep . . .
     Lady *Day* . . . Lady Di . . . sad goodbye.

283. Being a *maso*chist, alas, was her lot,
      Need for *pain* put her mate on the spot;
      They a*voided* malfunction
      By para*dox*ical injunction:
      He *hurt* her by hurting her . . . or not.

284. In his *every*day life John's a giant,
But in *private* John's just a half-pint;
There's a *dom*inatrix
Who wears *boots* that he licks
And has *rules* with which he's quite compliant.

Clumsy *Donna*, John's dominatrix,
Had a *very* large bag full of tricks;
Not some *tricks* that she'd play,
But dead *clients* she'd slay,
Whom she *damaged* . . . and then couldn't fix.

Once, while *role* playing Master and Slave,
John, with *death*, had a very close shave;
So he *said* to his Mistress,
"*Play* Damsel in Distress . . . ."
Now John's *some*body Donna must save.

285. Are you *sure* that you've got a G-spot?
    I've been *poking* around quite a lot,
    And *though* I can't find it
    I *really* don't mind it,
    I've found *lots* of places it's not.

286. Back-to-*back*, a new sexual position,
    Re*quires* a special condition:
    You've no *need* to be supple,
    But you'll *need* one more couple . . .
    To *con*summate a quartet coition.

287. A *New* Orleans 'house' was demolished
     And some *practices* therein were abolished:
     Men can *still* wine and dine
     Or *get* a shoe shine
     But can *no* longer get their knobs polished.

288. An old *Patriarch*, haunted with grief,
     Felt his *name* undermined his belief;
     Although *hard* to arrange it
     He *managed* to change it
     From *A*braham to . . . Abra<u>beef</u>.

289. A Greek *guy* and his gal tried to score
     But could *go* just so far and no more
     Since his *wife* and her lovers
     Had *used* all his rubbers . . .
     Thus *winning* the new Trojan War.

290. Between *her* and The Church grew a schism:
     She *violated* her catechism
     'Cause she'd *too* many offspring
     And *more* in the offing;
     Well . . . *not* All God's Chillun Got Rhythm.

291. A foot *fetishist* evoked all his pity
     When they *got* to the real nitty-gritty:
     She'd at *last* get her rocks off
     By taking his socks off
     And *tickling* his toes with her titty.

292. Dos her*manos* named Sancho and Pancho,
     Worked as *gauchos* on El Grande Rancho
     As *they* left the campus
     To *work* on the pampas
     Their *honcho* gave each one a poncho.

293. With sex *viewed* through puritanic prisms
      And *spoken* of in vague euphemisms,
      I'm so *glad* we found out
      Just what *it's* all about
      And re*ceived* our erotic Baptisms.

      Gals of *yore* could admire-a man's shoulder,
      But to*day's* gals are quite a bit bolder:
      They'll say, *"He's* good in bed."
      If he *gives* them good head
      And if *he* is much younger . . . not older.

294. When you *die,* being buried will show
     That you're *headed* for Hell down below;
     But *if* you're cremated,
     You'll *feel* elated:
     As *smoke*, up to Heaven you'll go.

     Death is *coming*, I don't know just when.
     Maybe *It's* down the road, 'round the bend;
     But I've *got* lots to do,
     Hope Death *waits* till I'm through
     And____!!!

Edwards Brothers Malloy
Thorofare, NJ USA
March 25, 2014